The *Call*

Also by David Spangler

The Call

David Spangler

Introduction by W. Brugh Joy M.D.

Lorian Press
Camano Island, WA
2015

The Call

Lorian Press
686 Island View Dr.
Camano Island, WA 98282

ISBN: 978-0-936878-84-3

Spangler/David
The Call/David Spangler
Introduction by W. Brugh Joy M.D.

First Lorian Press Edition 2015
Original Edition Riverhead Books 1996

Printed in the United States of America

Lorian.org

Acknowledgments

I happily want to acknowledge my friend and colleague of nearly twenty years, Dr. Brugh Joy. Were it not for his invitation in 1978 to create a New Year's conference with him, this book would not exist.

It also would not exist without the faith and vision of my editors, Susan Petersen and Wendy Carlton, and my agent, Ned Leavitt. I also want to thank Kim Seidman for a wonderful job of copyediting, keeping my ideas clear while retaining a conversational tone throughout the book, repetitions and all! Thank you all for your support.

This book grew out of a talk I gave at the New Year's conference, which Brugh and I sponsored every year at the Asilomar Conference Center in California on the shore of the Pacific Ocean. This was a most unusual and energetic conference, filled annually with mystery, fun, outstanding presenters, and deep spirit. Several thousand people have attended in the years we ran it, and the substance of this book definitely grows out of the love I have felt from all these people throughout all these years. Thank you to each of you.

It has been a calling and a privilege to serve you at that special time when one year emerges from another, and hope, vision, and the power of the call are vibrant and alive in each of us.

*This one is for Julie
and the love that is
the call between us.*

Introduction

If David Spangler's book on the spiritual call were conventional, my introduction would begin as follows:

> The holy call is a revelation, an inner prompting, a vision, causing an individual to turn from a personal, self-centered, and superficially expressed life to that of a servant of the divine.

> The numinosity of such a transcendent call is often of such a magnitude that the individual experiences a rupture of his or her life. He or she is cast into a vaster consciousness, and often acts with the sense of extreme vulnerability and wounding brought on by the leaving behind—and therefore the betrayal of everything that had previously held primary value in the individual's personal life. The members of the family, circle of friends, professional

colleagues, and organizations threatened by such a disruption may exert extreme pressure to reform the called one. And, failing that, to ignore or, worse yet, to cast out the "misguided" individual.

The effect of the spiritual call—to cause a transformation, of varying degrees, of both the individual and the collective—completes the divine intention.

Part of David's discourse reflects his experience of the accepted spiritual call. Yet, much more important, his writing opens our eyes and our hearts to a more profound and unconventional understanding of the spiritual call—one that gives each of us the opportunity to explore a wonder-filled appreciation of how divinely inspired, and therefore "called," the commonly experienced aspects of our lives actually are.

For me, David's ability to reveal the sacred calling that lies behind our lives with clarity of thought, playful humor, and a most remarkable aura of spiritual love makes

even more divinely delightful this contribution to personal
and communal spiritual transformation.

W. BRUGH JOY, M.D.

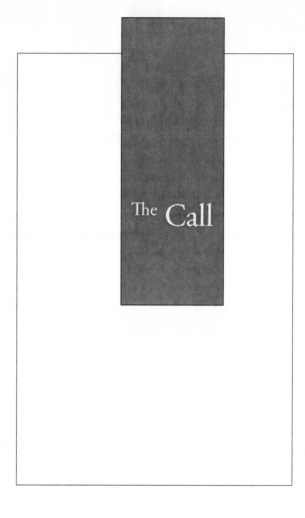

The Call

There is a need we all feel to be part of something larger than ourselves. So much of our energy as human beings goes into finding that connection with something larger. We have a deep need for identity. Belonging to something larger is a way of telling ourselves, "This is who I am."

From this quest for identity—for a sense of who we are, why we are here, and what life is about—have emerged religions, philosophies, and even human civilization as a whole. It is certainly present as a driving force in our individual lives. If you took a moment and looked into your heart right now, you would find this same quest for identity.

It is a quest that never quite gets answered. Who are you? At any given time, there are various ways you might answer this question: "I am a Democrat"; "I am a Republican"; "I am an American"; "I am white"; "I am black"; "I am a woman"; "I am a man"; "I am _____" and you can fill in the blank with whatever you wish. Yet there is always, somewhere in the background, a lurking question that asks, 'Yes, but . . . are you sure? Is this really the whole story of who you are? Do you really know who you are?" And this question is a quiet anxiety that can live within us and color our days.

There are a couple of ways to respond to this inner question. One way is to deny that it is there and to hold ever more tightly to the particular answer with which you have filled in the blank. This defensiveness, though, may only increase the anxiety, for the question from which it springs is now perceived as a threat.

The other option is to say, "Well, for right now, provisionally, to the best of my knowledge, I am this. But I am open to further information. I am open to further discovery. I have set boundaries with my answer, but they are permeable. They can be expanded toward new possibilities." This response can decrease the anxiety, or at least channel it constructively, for now the question behind it is seen as an opportunity.

In our world today, we see this question of identity played out between two types of people. There are those people who say, "I want to answer this question of who I am once and for all. I don't want to be troubled by this issue anymore; I don't want the anxiety it brings, so don't you dare say anything to me that will challenge my answer."

Then there are those other people who say, "Let me explore. Let me go boldly where no identity has gone before. What are the endless reaches of who I am and who I can become? Let me go and see."

For me, the issue of the "call" falls squarely into this context of identity.

When I was a teenager, my parents and I went to see a movie that quite strongly affected me at the time. The movie was *A Man Called Peter*, and it was a film biography of Peter Marshall, who, for a number of years, was the chaplain of the United States Senate. I don't remember much of the film now, but one scene does stand out. Marshall, who was Scottish, is stumbling across the moors late one night in the middle of a storm. He comes to the edge of a cliff, and he almost goes over because he can't see it in the dark. But he hears a voice. Something says to him, "Stop!" And he stops. Then the storm clears enough for him to see that he is on the edge of this precipice and that if he had not stopped when he did, he would have plunged over to his death. When he realizes that his life has been saved by this voice, it is as if the experience expands within him, filling him with a sense of grace, and he has a feeling of being called by God.

To talk about one's vocation is not uncommon among those who become clergy. I have talked to many who have said, "I was called to the vocation of being a minister." In the same sense, Peter Marshall felt called. Watching this on the screen, this notion of being called by something larger than yourself, struck me very deeply.

It wasn't very much longer after that, a few years only, that I felt my own calling to enter a path of life different from the one I had been on up to that time, a path that has taken me in a different direction from what I had anticipated. I suppose the reason that episode in the film about Peter Marshall affected me so deeply was that a part of me was anticipating my own calling and was undergoing a preparation of soul for when it would occur.

I was not stumbling across the moors of Scotland when it happened. I was, however, stumbling through my dormitory room in college! I was in my third year of working toward a Bachelor of Science degree in biochemistry. I wanted to be—I knew I was going to be—a genetic engineer. I wanted to work with the chemical basis of life and identity; the idea of doing that really turned me on (which, I suppose, is why I have ended up with four kids). I did not come to the edge of a precipice, but I did hear an inner voice that said, "It is now time for you to leave college and begin a spiritual work."

Right.

No way was I leaving college. This was in the middle of the sixties, and the Vietnam war was going full blast. I had a draft deferment. I was moving toward the career that I wanted. I was making straight A's in my classes. Frankly, I was a nerd. I had my slide rule, which I carried like a sword in a sheath on my belt. When I'd meet other nerds in the corridors of the science department, we'd whip out our slide rules and joust! How could life get airs better than that? Why would 1 want to change'?

But all my life I'd had this other side of me that knew a spiritual realm existed and that I could enter it from time to time and communicate with the beings who lived within it. About the same time that I was finishing up high school, I discovered that this talent was not a normal part of everyone else's life, that most other people did not experience the existence of inner worlds and nonphysical realities. Through my parents, I had begun meeting other people who did share this talent: channels and clairvoyants and psychics. From them I discovered a language and a set of images for talking about the kinds of inner experiences I had had growing up but which I had not known how to talk about. But all this was on the side. It was like a hobby. It was something I did not think about a lot. I was going to be a scientist who just happened, on the side, to be connected to the inner worlds.

However, the inner worlds had another path in mind for me. They said, "Time for you to leave school."

I said, "No."

I've always felt quite free to say no to the inner worlds, but they feel equally free to say no back to me if it seems necessary. Apparently, this time it was necessary, So about a week after I said no, I literally felt as if somebody had thrown a switch and turned my mind off. I went to class as usual, but now nothing the instructor said made sense. Nothing that I read made sense. It was like I had had a lobotomy. For a couple of months, I watched my grades plummet, until finally the penny dropped and I thought, *I don't think I'm supposed to be here. I'm supposed to be somewhere else.* I left the university,

At which point my mind turned back on again.

That was how I was called. I share this story because the image of that call, of having had that experience, stayed with me for years and acted within me as a form of identity. When confusing times came and things in my life seemed uncertain and bewildering, I could still say, "Well, I was called. I have a vocation to be an itinerant, freelance mystic." This image of being called became one of the important ways that I filled in the blank when the question "Who am I?" would arise. Saying "I am the person who was called by spirit" became an answer to the question of my identity.

Over the years, however, I've learned there is much more to the idea of the call than simply answering the question "Who am I?" To explain this, I would like to make a distinction between a "call" and a summoning.

I believe that for many of us, when we think of the call and of being called, we are actually thinking of being summoned. 'When you are summoned, there is implicit in this idea a sense of direction. I am summoned to do something or to go somewhere specific. I am summoned to dinner. I am summoned to my work. I am summoned to the courthouse. I get a summons!

A call, however, need not be that specific. It need not offer a definite sense of vocation or direction. In fact, some of the most powerful calls that we may receive in our lives, the calls that come from the deepest places in ourselves, are not summoning but are more like awakenings. They call us to attention.

How often we have the experience of somebody calling our name and immediately our attention is heightened. We say, "Yes?" or "Here I am!" or whatever response is appropriate. The call may not carry with it any kind of implicit direction. The person doing the calling may simply want to know if we're here. For example, my youngest boy gets home from school. He comes in the door, and he calls out, 'Mom? Dad?" He knows we're there, but he wants to be reassured that we're there. So from wherever I am in the house, I call out in response and let him know where I am and what I'm doing, usually something like, "I'm over here. I'm at my computer, writing." (Someday I'd like to call out, "I'm lying on the sofa, eating sinfully rich mint chocolates and watching television!) The call may not be doing anything other than establishing a presence, determining that we're really here, that we've "shown up," as anthropologist and spiritual teacher Angeles Arrien would say. So the call may not be to a specific duty, but to an awareness of what the moment asks of us. It is a call to pay attention.

In the 1960s a most important scientific discovery was made: the discovery of the background radiation of the universe. This discovery showed that in all directions of the sky, there is a uniform distribution of radiation, which was determined to be the residue of the Big Bang, that moment when the universe emerged. This discovery is important because it furnished empirical evidence in support of what, up until then, had been simply a theory that the universe was formed from an unknown state by a great explosion, the Big Bang, after which it began to expand very rapidly and eventually form the cosmos as we know it, leaving behind this uniform background radiation.

Well, in a similar way, there is a background call that is in all of us and, indeed, in all things. This is the call of love, the original radiation of creation.

In the Christian tradition, we are told that God so loved the world that He gave His only son to be born as a human person to perform a task of planetary redemption. This is proof that we are loved—the world is loved—in a deep and profound way.

Much as the background radiation proves there was a Big Bang at the beginning, the Incarnation proves there was a Big Love there as well. Other religious traditions have similar sacrificial images testifying to the all-pervading, all-encompassing love of the sacred for creation. In Hindu teachings, for example, God does not give a son, but gives itself; the universe is born of a great sacrifice by which the deity dismembers itself so to speak. Out of this dismembering, all the worlds are born.

Implicit in these teachings of sacrifice, of the death of gods on behalf of humanity and all the worlds of creation, is the knowledge that we are valuable, that we are loved, that we are important. Again, this suggests that there is a background call of which all other calls are an echo: the call to respond to the love that created us by being lovers of all that is created.

It has been assumed, with some justification, that science has removed humanity from the center of things. It has placed us way out on the fringes of our galaxy and said that we all are random accidents in an uncaring and meaningless universe. But this perception is changing. Over the past decade, new theories of cosmology and creation have been developed that say that, because of the way the universe is structured, intelligent life had to emerge. The "anthropic principle" states that the universe is designed to give birth to beings like us. So even though we exist on the rim of our galaxy, in a backwater corner of the Milky Way, nowhere near the center of things, we are still the object of the exercise. Consciousness, sentiency, mind, heart, awareness, life: all are at the center of the universe's direction. Science now appears to be saying, "Yes, at the heart of the universe is a process that increasingly looks like it can do no other than produce beings like us in whom the cosmos can become self-reflective and self-conscious."

So just as in the religious traditions there is a sense that we are valued and important, there is a similar idea now emerging in science, which in many ways is the religion of the twentieth century. We are valued, for we are the consciousness of the universe incarnating itself and becoming aware.

Another scientific discovery, the hologram, gives rise to yet another important insight: Everything that is part of a larger whole replicates within itself the essence of that larger whole. The whole is contained in the part, even as the part is contained in the whole.

Thus, if God—the cosmic whole—so loved the world and the cosmos that He gave His only son for its salvation, as the Christian tradition states, or if the Ultimate Being so loved the idea and potential of creation that it gave its own self to be the body of a universe, then that act of loving surrender and sacrifice lives in us as well.

We are also giving ourselves to the world, to one another, to the future because we love the world; we are participating in that great sacrifice from which worlds are born and, if necessary, redeemed.

So, we are here on earth in part because of love, because the world has value, and we have value, and we wish to nourish and succor this. We are here because of that unique gift that only each of us can give to the world, each in his or her own way. I cannot love the world for you or sacrifice you for its well-being. Only you can do that for yourself, as only I can do that for myself. Only each of us can give the unique gift of love inherent in our individuality

We are here because the Big Love recognizes our value and knows what we can become, what we can give, what we can do that will bring new life, new vision, new spirit, new love to the world.

This is the primal call.

This is the background call in the lives of each of us, like the background radiation of the universe: the call to treasure and value and love one another and all the other creatures and things of the earth. It is the call to acknowledge and to act from that knowledge that each person is just as valued and just as loved as the next, and all are invited to participate in the communion of that love.

When I was just entering my teens, I came to meet and know a number of people who were psychics and channels, because of my parents' interest in metaphysics and parapsychological phenomena. Some of these people were channels of great skill and integrity because they were *persons* of skill and integrity first, with a deep attunement to the sacred and to the honoring of life. Unfortunately, however, they were rare. Most of the channels I met at that time did not have much skill or real attunement, nor did they have the integrity to admit it. As individuals, they were driven by their egos, interested in adulation, control, and power, while not particularly interested in the well-being or liberation of the people who came to consult with them. They were not people to emulate. As a consequence, I developed a strong bias against channels and channeling, for I felt the whole process had a negative effect on a person's character and generally did not attract a particularly spiritual level of contact with the other side.

I was surprised, then, when I was approached by a spirit being one morning who said, in effect, "Well, here I am to work with you!" Now, I have been aware of spirit beings and the existence of non-physical dimensions all my life, though I never thought much about it until, as a teenager, I began to meet others who had similar experiences. What surprised me was that one of these beings had specifically sought me out and said that we were going to work together.

I called this being "John," because I liked that name. It captured for me the essence of a loving spirit, and this being was, and is, if nothing else, profoundly loving. When John said he wanted to work with me, however, the only model I had for that kind of work was channeling, so at first I was reluctant. But he assured me that he was not interested in my going into some trance state and becoming a channel either. So I agreed to the partnership.

Two years after that, however, John came to me one day and said, "We would like you to do readings for people." He wanted me to experience being a psychic or intuitive consultant, drawing on his help to do so. My first response was, "You must be kidding! No way am I going to do that." For again my image of what that meant was to be a channel. "No," he replied, "we really think it would be a good idea and important for your understanding and growth, but we agree, you will do so in full consciousness. No trance states!"

For all of my contrariness, I have learned to trust John. So I eventually said. "All right, I will do it." But I had a great deal of trepidation and, I honesty admit, some misplaced pride and snobbery in me that said. "I'm not going to be like one of those channels!"

Nevertheless, I hung out my shingle, so to speak, and people started coming to me for readings. This went on for about three years. It was an eye-opening experience for me to see how willing people were to give their power away to me because they felt I could access another dimension of life. With no justification other than that I could speak with a spirit being, they were willing to turn me into an expert and surrender their free will to me and to John, asking that we make important choices for them. But neither John nor I would ever take their power. When they wanted him to tell them what to do, he would give their power back by saying something like, "All right. You've asked this question. Now, let's discuss it together because you know what you need to do. You may not be admitting it or you may not have recognized it because you just haven't thought it through yet. So let's talk about it and see what choices you would make." Then John would discuss the issue with them, adding his perspective to enlarge and clarify their own until, in fact, they discovered that they did know what to do.

Interestingly, the one question that people most often asked, and the one question that was the most difficult for him to answer in most cases, was, "What is my calling? Why am I here? What am I supposed to do in my life?" John's reaction to that question was intriguing, a kind of amused puzzlement, with the amusement directed mainly toward himself for his failure to fully understand why people asked this question. I believe that John wanted me to become an intuitive counselor for a while so that not only could I learn some lessons (and get over my bias against channels) but so that he could learn some as well. He wanted to learn what people wanted and what was happening in the human condition. So, when people asked him, "What is my calling?" he would in turn ask me, "Why is this person asking this question? What does it mean? What are they seeking?" Through our intimate link of mind and soul, I could see what John saw: this person's calling was simply to be himself or herself. The call was to discover in the here and now, in all the ramifications and details of his or her individual life, how to be his or her essence, which was love. In other words, what John saw was the primal background call, the call to love oneself, to love others, and to love that presence and mystery we name the sacred. Basically, for John, every person's calling was to heighten and clarify the background call so that it would come into the foreground of his or her life. It was like heightening the background radiation of the universe.

Occasionally someone would come to see us, and John would say, "This person has come into incarnation to do something specific, and this is what it is." But that response was very rare. Usually John would say, "Let's take a look at your life, because in its texture and content, you will discover why you are here. The fact that you are in incarnation is itself a gift both to you and from you to the earth, and you are here because the earth has called to you. The earth has called to you at this time in its history because it wants souls who can expand their powers of lovingness and compassion, souls who can begin to look beyond certain fixed and habitual positions, certain traditional perspectives, and say, 'Is there more?' The earth needs people who can say, 'Yes, there is more.' Not just more in the way of knowledge or inventions or wisdom or revelations, but more compassion, more gentleness and sweetness, more caring, more love, more valuing of one another. That is your mission, and it is of the highest, for it is nothing other than the mission of manifesting the spirit of the Beloved in your life."

Many people know of me through my association with the spiritual community of Findhorn in northern Scotland. From 1970 to 1973, I was a co-director of this center, along with Peter and Eileen Caddy and Dorothy Maclean, the three original founders. The community is located on a beach on the Findhorn Bay, about forty miles east of famous Loch Ness, and it is most well known for its miraculous garden grown on sand dunes and rocky soil, where no such garden should really exist—certainly not in such vigor and abundance. Their secret is good compost plus active spiritual cooperation with the angels.

When I arrived, this community was only a small group of about fifteen people. They had gathered together not only to work with the garden, but also in response to numerous prophecies from the sixties about an impending planetary event that would initiate a New Age. They were preparing themselves for that transformation, for the birth of a New Age.

One day Peter Caddy came to me with a letter from a group in Australia. It basically said that on a particular day in 1971, all hell was going to break loose. There would be nuclear war and earthquakes and the polar ice caps were going to slip and the earth would shift on its axis . . . . in other words, one of those days when you know you should stay in bed. Out of this holocaust, the survivors would then rise and be led by spiritual forces into a New Age. After reading this letter to me, Peter said, "What am I going to do with this? This group has supported us in the past, and now they have received this prophecy and they want me to put it out on our mailing list so people can get prepared." And I said, "Well, my own inner attunement says that nothing like this is going to happen. This is pure fantasy and paranoid projection."

Then I added, "What is it that we would need to do if we were living in the New Age? We'd still have to eat. We'd still have to cook. We'd still have children to raise, marriages to nourish, values to express. What really is so different about the New Age? Basically, we'd have to do the same things, express the same lovingness, embody the same integrity, and take care of one another and our world in the New Age as we do now. So what is stopping us from doing that now instead of waiting for some event or prophecy to give us permission to be what we already are? I think it would be better to assume that whatever the great event is that all these groups are awaiting, it has already taken place and we are already in the New Age. We don't have to wait anymore. We can get on with creating a New Age in our everyday lives.

So many people in those days were caught up in thinking, what are the alternatives? What could he different about our world? But I think the important question is, "What would be the same?" Because if we start with what is the same, we can go from there; we can focus upon how we do what is already at hand for us to do. The differences will emerge as they need to. What is the same is that I still need to learn how to be loving to you.

At times that seems like such a huge task. What does it mean to be loving? How can I be loving? But it so often comes down to such simple things as, "Can I value you? Can I be courteous to you? Can I honor you? Can I treat you with integrity?" We think of love as an attitude and at times struggle to have it, but in many ways it is a behavior. It is what we do.

What is the behavior of being loving?

In one of the loveliest Arthurian stories, Sir

Gawain, a knight of the Round Table, agrees to marry Ragnal, a most hideously ugly hag in exchange for her telling the king a secret that will save him from death. The wedding is held, and all the kingdom has pity for this handsome and gallant knight who is marrying someone so horrible in both appearance and manners.

After Gawain and his bride retire to their wedding chambers, she excuses herself to slip into something more comfortable, while he climbs into bed, prepared to do his conjugal duty with this hag. Then, out from the curtains steps a stunningly beautiful young woman, the "fairest woman in the land."

Gawain is dumbfounded. "Where is my wife? What have you done to her?"

"I am your wife," the woman replies. Then she tells how an evil sorcerer had put an enchantment upon her so that she shifted from being rapturously beautiful to being repulsively ugly.

"Now," Ragnall says to Gawain, "you have a choice. As my husband, you must decide if you want me beautiful by night for your pleasure, and ugly by day, knowing that people will pity you; or beautiful by day, so people will honor you, and ugly by night, which will bring you no pleasure. Which do you want? You decide."

All husbands should take note of this, for Gawain proves his wisdom as a man and his smarts as a husband. He says, "This is not for me to choose. I want you to be the way you want to be. It is your choice."

He gives her back her power. Gawain does not try to decide Ragnall's life for her. He says, "You are the powerful one. It is your choice, not mine." With that, the spell on her is broken and she is beautiful all the time. He honors her sovereignty, and that frees her to be her true self.

That to me is loving behavior: giving back power and honoring the integrity of another. It is valuing who the other is. That is a behavior that says, "God loved the world, so He (or She) sent you here, too. You are important. I want to honor you because of this importance. I want to honor your sovereignty. I want to treasure who you are."

Love is not just an attitude, a feeling, or an energy. It is a behavior. Sometimes people say, "Well, if I just behave as if I were loving, but I don't really feel it, I'm being hypocritical. It isn't honest." In point of fact, when you behave as if you are loving, that behavior can invoke the attitude itself: energy follows action. This is one of the principles behind magic and ritual. You form circles, beat drums, light candies, chant chants, dance about, or do whatever you do in a ritualistic way in order to invoke or raise a quality of energy. But if you already have that energy why go through all the fuss? You do so in the expectation that by ritualistically acting out, you will create a vessel of imagination that will invoke and hold whatever essence or quality that you wish. You act first, and the inner reality follows. Your action is the call.

If I say, "Well, yes, I'll behave in a loving way. I just have to get my attitude in the right place. I have to get my heart in the right place. I have to get my head on straight. I have some more internal processing to do first. I'm not really there yet," then that call won't come. I am not performing the magic ritual. I am discounting the power of outer reality and behavior to affect my inner state.

The call actually comes from the person standing in front of you, who in their heart of hearts is saying, "Will you be kind to me? Will you value me? I am valuable, after all. Will you honor me? Will you see the sacred in me, the sovereignty in me?" It is my action in response to that call that draws me into a loving space. It is what opens me to experience the background call of the universe.

This background call summons all of us out of the substance of the sacred to enter into manifestation. Humans are called specifically into incarnation in this world which loves us and wants us. And we want to be here in the most fundamental way. We wish to be here. There may be many reasons for that, but at the core, it is because our souls responded to that call of love. It is because life itself is a calling, a dialogue between the earth and ourselves as we each strive to fulfill the potentials with which God has graced us.

That was my spirit friend John's perception of us. He saw each of us as walking answers to a call: a sacred call to enter manifestation, a planetary call to help the earth, and a communal call to empower and co-create with one another. He would often say, therefore, when someone would ask about his or her calling, "Your calling is to be here. There is no higher mission, for each of us is a gateway that can open to allow the Beloved to step through. To give expression to the Beloved, to be that gateway, is why the universe appeared. It is the ultimate Call."

The primal call is the call to love. It is a call to be loving and to accept love in return. It calls us beyond rhetoric and beyond excuses. It calls us out of ourselves.

There are many things that call us out of ourselves and, in the moment we transcend our own boundaries, open us to the presence of the Beloved, to the background call of the cosmos. For example, a gift or talent that we possess can draw us to others and to expressing ourselves in connective ways. It might be a gift for music or for painting, for crafting the written word or for weaving stories on film. This talent is like a call, for it draws us to a vocation or at least an expression of an art that not only uplifts us, but finds its fullness in being shared. On the other hand, it can be a subtler gift, such as for being a great listener, one whose silence and empathy becomes a call in itself to draw out from others the toxins of despair or the sweet wines of enthusiasm and dreams. It could be a gift for relating to children or for crafting a loving household or for working with persons who are physically or mentally challenged. Having such a gift becomes a call that summons us to special relationships and creates open spaces in which others may grow and thrive.

Likewise, responsibilities and commitments may be calls, drawing us out when we prefer to be left alone or to go in different direction. I have been very blessed in my marriage in that every day is like the first day my wife and I were together. But as a spiritual teacher, I have worked with people whose relationships have wandered into dry and dusty places. In these deserts of the heart, it is easy to look to other people and other places where sweet water seems to flow; but there is part of us that has the power to cross these deserts and, by so doing, make them bloom again. It is the power of love, integrity, and even sacrifice, and it is our commitment that can call it forth from within us.

Our lives are woven from a melody of such calls that draw us out and help us to define ourselves.

Now, I want to reiterate the distinction between a summons and a call. I can call you for no other reason than that I love you and want your attention, or I'm in a friendly mood, or I wish you to be aware of me. I'm not asking anything of you. How often do you call up a friend just to say hello? But a summons carries with it a sense of purpose, mission, and identity. Many of us feel a desire for that kind of summons, something that will ennoble us, put us to the test, and give meaning to our lives.

There are summonses implicit in the primal call; they can take the form of responsibilities that are woven into the holistic fabric of life, and, like social responsibilities, they call us into engagement with the world. Traditionally, some of these summonses have been identified by religion, perhaps to such an extent that we think of them as religious prescriptions and not as something inherent in life itself, So, for example, if I say, "I am called to be my brother's or sister's keeper," that seems like a religious maxim. However, on a deeper level than religious law, we may perceive that because of the intimate connections that unite us in a universal ground of being, I really am your keeper, not for any religious, moral, or ethical reason, as society defines these terms, but because we share an extended body together. We are part or a wholeness. Your well-being is my wellbeing; in keeping you, I am also keeping myself.

Becoming aware of this connection and fulfilling it is a summons. I am summoned by a primal condition of life itself that seeks to maintain the integrity of its own wholeness. This summons me to be responsive to the incarnation and well-being of my fellow beings.

When we think of being summoned, we may think of something that defines a vocation for us and sends us out on a quest or mission. This brings us up against mythic images prevalent in Western culture—the images of the heroic quest, the hero, and the heroine. When we are summoned, in other words, it is not just to do the dishes. We are summoned, we feel, because something in the universe says, "You have hero material in you!" A summons, we believe, asks us to go on a quest. It places us in a mythic context.

It is interesting that in our culture, when we think of a hero or heroine, we think of a solitary individual: the lonely heroine, the man on the white horse. What we have forgotten is that the hero is a collective entity, that is, he is a servant of the collective. The hero is the growing edge of the community, the part that explores, that goes out into the unknown, uncovers a mystery, discovers new information or skills, gains new assets or allies, and then brings all these things back for the benefit of the whole. The heroic quest is not fulfilled until the hero returns; it has no meaning until the hero gives the gift or the wisdom back to his or her community. The value of the hero lies in the uplifting of the whole community.

This is also true of the shaman. Traditionally, the shaman exists as the healing servant of the community. The shaman is a person who sacrifices himself or herself to be a vessel for spirit, to act on behalf of a larger collective. In a way, the shaman renders his or her personal life. He or she may do heroic deeds, but they are not done for personal gain or even in the interest of identity. They are done to benefit the community.

But in the West we have another image as well—that of the adept. This image, whether embodied in the form of a magician, an inventor, a scientist, or an entrepreneur, seems to me to be part of the deep mythic structure of Western consciousness. The adept is the man or woman who possesses a power derived from individual effort through study, learning, and action. He or she may act for others but remains essentially a loner, with independent motives. By contrast, the shaman's or hero's power is defined by its community context. The idea of this person being someone who would go off and act on his or her own behalf for individual glory and reward is really alien to the primal image of the shaman or the hero.

But in our culture, we've had an arc of cultural development over many centuries, leading to the development of the individual and valuing the notion of the individual. Our culture has been called to discover and understand the mystery of individuality and the nature of solitary power.

Because of our focus on individuality, we understand the nature of a summons as something that singles us out and gives us individual meaning and importance. That is why we long for it. It gives us a unique identity. What could be more meaningful and individualizing than to feel singled out by some higher force that says, "You have a special quality, and because of this, I am tapping you on the shoulder to do a special work"? And then we are sent on a heroic quest or a shaman's journey, or something equally adventuresome and glorious.

The call to individuality is vital, and at times there are tasks to be done in the world that fall specifically upon us to do. Yet there is another call that is equally important. It is the call to integrate our individuality back into the community, into communion with humanity. It is the call not to separate but to blend, to contribute, to co-create, and to serve. If the primal call of love summons us to be ourselves, it also summons us to be part of a larger wholeness.

When we feel called, when we feel the summoning of spirit, there are two responses that can arise in us. One is fear. The other is ego.

The fear says, "Gee, I don't know. It's lonely out there, and people who go out on quests like these or answer these kinds of summonses get crucified, they get killed, they get ostracized. I could fail. Then what would happen?"

These fears are real. Success is not guaranteed. Others may not understand. We will probably encounter many kinds of opposition. So we may wish to ask ourselves, when we are yearning to be called, "Do I really want a call?" For the call may not come either at a time or in a way that we would choose. I certainly did not choose for my call to come when I was twenty and in my third year of college. Why couldn't it have waited a year until I got my degree? So we may want to ask ourselves, "Am I prepared for what a call might bring?" Because if I summon a summoning, if I invoke a call through my desire, the very worst thing I can do is then say no to it.

If I invoke the energy to me and give it no place to go, then I am stuck with it. I have to find a way to give it back gracefully or do something with it. And actually, you can give it back gracefully. You can say no to a call, but you have to say no in a way that appreciates where you are at the moment. You can say, "No, I don't feel I can do this. I'm not ready. I would like to be more prepared, therefore I will undertake that preparation. I will undertake a discipline to understand more fully the nature of this call and why it came to me, so that I will be prepared the next time it comes."

Of course, that which summoned you (or which you summoned) may not be satisfied with this. It may say, "Come on! You can do it. You can do it, and if you don't, you will always wonder. You will look back with regret and be sorry for a lost opportunity."

So, a summons can bring fear, especially if I invoked it without really being serious about its consequences, but just because I wanted some higher power to take an interest in me. If I am going to invoke a summons, though, then what I ought to do is to be clear about what conditions, if any, I might desire. Traditionally, we believe that a summons from a higher power requires unconditional surrender from us, and often it does—at least it requires unconditional acceptance of the energy that comes with that summoning. But before it comes, we can set forth some conditions. We can ask ourselves, "All right, am I ready for a calling, and if so, what am I really ready for? What are my parameters? What are my conditions?" Be prepared, though, that the source of a summons may have a different and more expanded notion of just what we are capable of, and may push us to go beyond our conditions.

Actually, any higher power that may send us a call is more interested in getting accomplished whatever the job is; therefore, it will usually not ask us to do anything that is truly beyond our capabilities. What is more likely is that we will receive a series of summonses, each asking a little bit more of us, each building on the other.

In this way, I take a step, and when I am successful, I have confidence. I have a sense of trust, both in myself and in the source of the calling. I am then able to take a bigger step. This is the approach I would use if I were training to run a marathon. I would not get up from my relatively sedentary life writing at a computer and go out and run twenty-six miles all in one go. I would train for this event, or I would suffer the consequences. Spiritual paths are very much like that. You train. You go to the edge of what you think you can do. Then you push that edge a bit, get comfortable, then push it some more. Pretty soon you discover that that edge just keeps moving back.

The other force besides fear that can arise when we feel summoned is ego. Now, I believe that a healthy ego is a good thing, or at least a neutral thing. It provides an inner structure that is specific and grounded for spirit to work with. But there is a shadow side to ego that we all are aware—egotism or self-centeredness—which is actually a lack of imagination, trust, and faith in oneself. What I am doing when I give way to egotism is establishing certain boundaries and the images associated with that boundary, and saying that this is what I'll settle for. Yet I can guarantee you that God's image of you is much greater than anything you may conceive of for yourself or about yourself, even in your most heightened state of egotistic inflation.

This is because as an ego, you can work only with

what you already know. After all, the essence of egotism is that you feel only you have the answer, only you really know what's what, so you are not open to outside perspectives. Thus, your fantasies, ego-projections, and megalomania, however grandiose they may seem, are limited by the extent of your knowledge, your understanding, and your imagination. What the Sacred perceives is what you don't know yet, and may never know about yourself or your world as long as your ego maintains the boundary of its sense of superiority. It takes real humility to go through that boundary and to challenge your sense that you know it all.

We all go through the I-know-it-all stage, usually as teenagers. It is a phase we hopefully outgrow as we learn more and discover how much we don't know. But some part of us may never outgrow it, and if that part becomes dominant, it turns our ego into a barrier to learning. The function and characteristic of the ego—to provide a specific psychic structure that can ground the energy of our incarnation and give it shape and definition—becomes usurped. This shape then becomes a limit, trapped in its lack of imagination and its lack of willingness to embrace the unknown.

So, ego, when bounded in this way, is always a defensive measure. It arises from fear. It cannot admit that it might have weaknesses or limitations that make it vulnerable to life. It looks for ways of buttressing its feelings of superiority and, ultimately, its sense of safety. In this context, when I get a summons, I may think to myself, "Hey! I am being summoned by God! That makes me pretty special!"

Most people, including egotists, do not have particularly great self-images, something which the egotist seeks to hide even from himself. Receiving a summons allows me to cloak my ego in something that carries authority and weight. So I may then expand my initial response to a summons and say, "Because God has summoned me, which makes me special, I must be the new Christ. I must be the new Buddha. I must be a new prophet or savior."

We can go through a whole list of powerful images that tell the world how great we are. But the truth is that when we are summoned, it is not because we are great or special, but because we can give of ourselves to the world in some way. We are summoned to a task that is almost always a task of service. In some way, it will demand of us a surrender of our sense of self as well, because the flip side of every summons is transformation of the summonee. The hero and the shaman do not remain untouched by their quests; their transformations are part of the gifts they bring back. So a summons calls us to work and to serve in a way that prepares us for a new sense of self to develop, and to allow something that we don't yet know about ourselves to unfold in our lives.

We all know the challenges that arise in this culture when we overly identify with our work. We all know people who undergo deep psychological challenges when retirement comes or they're laid off. Their whole identities were wrapped around their work. "What I do is who I am," they have told themselves. "This is how I answer the question of my identity." We don't want this kind of identification with a summons or a call. We don't want it to define the entire meaning of our life. For even if we are summoned to do a task, that summons never *fully* defines or identifies us as God sees us. It identifies only an opportunity to contribute something to the collective.

It does not tell us who we are, for who we are in God's eyes is always so much more than the part of us that can accomplish a specific task.

If I long for a summons to come into my life, I should ask why. What need do I think it would fulfill? If I simply want something to do that will give me a sense of well-being, a sense of participation in the universe, a sense of being part of divinity or spirit, or a sense of value, I don't need to look far in my world. My culture is filled with needs and problems. I don't require God to tell me to look for ways of contributing to my society or being kind to those around me; I can discover those things for myself. My perception of the needs of others and my own compassion can be all the summons I really need.

The things I can do can be such simple things, but that does not make them unimportant. Our world grows out of simple things. I might feel summoned, for example, to look closely at myself every time I get angry, to see where the anger is coming from and ask whether it is an appropriate response. If it is an appropriate response, can I be angry in a mindful and loving way? Can I turn my anger from an explosion into a laser that cuts through something and produces a creative shift of behavior? Just doing that can be a transformative act.

For me, my kids are my gurus and teachers. There is absolutely no question about it. They are my mentors in dealing with issues like anger, for they have ways of pushing my buttons and surfacing unresolved stuff from my subconscious that would make the greatest psychiatrist green with envy. I have found myself at times totally surprised and ambushed by anger at something one of my kids has done. All at once I am in the middle of a rage like a storm that has swept up from over the horizon with no warning, and I am thinking, *Where did this come from?* because it is usually out of all proportion to what my child has done. ("What? You put your shoe on the wrong foot? Off with your head! ") So, in this instance, what is the call? The call is for me to look at this reaction. I am not called to get angry at myself for being angry. I am called to explore my reactions, to come to know myself better, to understand myself more deeply. I am called to discover why this reaction is part of me and what I can do about it. Sometimes in doing this, I have discovered habits that arose from my upbringing. My father rarely got angry; he is the sweetest and most loving man I know. But when anger came, there was no gradual buildup; he would just suddenly explode.

But I don't have to be like my dad. I don't have to perpetuate family habits. I don't have to parent the way my dad did, though I could certainly do worse, for he was a wonderful father. I, however, am my own unique self. I am my children's father, and we have a different relationship from that which I had with my father because we are different people. But I have to discover that difference and live up to it, for it is easier to fall back on habit. Though cultural advice and the experience of past generations can be helpful, the fact is that each interaction with any person is specific to that moment. It is a unique moment. I want to be mindful of the nature of that uniqueness and respond accordingly, appropriately. I want to be mindful that this moment has never happened before. I want to be mindful not to act out of habit.

Well, practicing that kind of mindfulness is a summoning. It is a call. It is a very simple kind of call, but it can be profound in its effects on those around me. If I don't have a call that says, "David, go out and be a healer," or, "David, run for the Presidency of the United States," or something specific and magnificent like that,

I can still look around and find all sorts of calls that are harkening to me, summoning me to be creative, loving, or simply attentive within my immediate vicinity.

If I begin to honor all these little calls, then I prepare the ground for a bigger call. I prepare it in such a way that when a bigger call comes, I can be like Cincinnatus, a Roman farmer who was called to become the head of the Roman Republic at a time of crisis. He was made dictator and given absolute power. And when the crisis was over, he gave back all the power and became a simple farmer again. He is a paradigm for somebody who is not seduced by the dark side of the force, who is not seduced by power or the egotistic glamour of his mission. When the big call comes, if I have prepared for it by answering and being mindful to little calls and to the background call, then the big call doesn't seem like a big call. It's just another call. It's another plow to put my hand to, another task to undertake, another situation in which to put my love. But if a big call comes and I haven't prepared myself by responding to little calls, little summonses, I will be more vulnerable to ego and fear, both of which may get in my way.

What happens if I never get a call? Well, that doesn't happen. We are always called. I hope I am making that clear. But I may never hear a voice or see an angel telling me what to do. I may never feel some force overwhelming my life and sending me forth on a quest or mission. I may never have some specific experience that tells me, "This is your identity. This is your destiny." The challenge, then, is, can I see past the lack of such phenomena to realize that I've already gotten, and have always gotten, the primal call? Can I realize that if I were not loved, and if love were not the gift I had to bring, I wouldn't be here on earth? It is love that brings me here, not karma, not past patterns to work out, but love and the fact that I have love to give.

Sometimes a call comes in stages. It builds throughout our lives. We may not even recognize the earlier stages for what they are; we may not hear them as a call. At Findhorn, one of the important figures who helped shape the community was Robert Ogilvie Crombie. When he was in his seventies, he suddenly became clairvoyant and began seeing nature spirits. This gift allowed him to make vital contributions to the development of the Findhorn garden. He could look back over his life and see a pattern of events and connections, all of which had prepared him for this work, though he had not realized it at the time. When the time came and Findhorn needed someone like him, he was ready, but the call that brought him to that point had actually begun to act in his life fifty years earlier, while he was still in college.

What happens if we get what we think is a call, and then sometime along the way it seems to fizzle? What happens if things don't work out the way we had anticipated? We may think of a summons or a call as an event. It happens at a certain time in our life and then everything from then on is an unfoldment of that calling. However, a call is more like an ongoing dialogue. It is a relationship that grows and changes and matures throughout a lifetime. It can be clear and resonant at times, and silent and subtle at other times.

There have been times in my life—sometimes very long periods of two or three years—when the energy of my calling seems to fade away and even disappear altogether. Then I am on my own, and I need to discover my connection with a deeper level of calling, one attuned to the primal call, the background call. In effect, I have to create my calling out of the love and wisdom and integrity of my own being.

It's a bit like going from high school, where everything is highly structured and lots of people tell us exactly what we need to do, to college, where we may find ourselves in an independent-study program that we have to design and monitor. I think that is how my spirit friend John sees the human experience. It is up to us to shape the curriculum. We pick the courses we want. We pick the teachers. We decide which degree we want. We decide. My oldest son is in a junior high school like that. It is an alternative school based on the principle that children will learn best and fastest when they choose the direction of their learning. He loves it. It's a challenge, for it puts a lot of responsibility upon him, but he is being exposed to a level of freedom that most of his peers are not. Sometimes he doesn't know what to do, just as sometimes we don't know what to do, but there are also times when he feels inwardly directed, just as we have those times as well.

So we feel ourselves in a flow, being guided, answering a call, and then, suddenly, it is gone. It's just gone. Whatever we felt doesn't have meaning anymore. What we were doing has lost its juice. We feel like we are in a limbo. What happened? Where did the call go? Did we lose it?

No. These times are also important in the dialogue or relationship that is the real call. These are the times when we reach into ourselves to supply the direction; it's our turn to speak. John used to say, "These are your most creative moments. It's easy to act and to feel like you are somebody when you feel you have an assignment. It is much more difficult to feel attuned, to feel part of something, to sense your identity when you do not feel you have any assignment, when you feel that you have nothing to do." Yet it is precisely at such times that we discover our true identity, not the identity shaped by a particular call or a particular work, but our soul, our essence, the very thing that we have to offer that is uniquely our own. It is this identity that the call is to in the first place; it is this identity that the call is intended to draw forth. Sometimes for this to happen, the call has to shut up.

When this happens, do we still feel called? Can we hear the deeper, background calls that lie under the more obvious summonings? Can we detect the living call that is our own soul—the call to be loved, to give love, to receive love; the call to be ourselves? The other calls, the calls from beyond us, will come back. In the meantime, it is nice to have the silence.

In working with spirit, it is wonderful to feel the flow of its energy, to feel summoned into life, to feel called to great things. But it is equally important to have times of silence, when we are thrust back upon ourselves. Then we need to listen. It's in this listening that we will hear the primal call, the background radiation of love and magic within the universe, the Big Bang of love that propels us into being, propels us to say, "I don't know what tomorrow brings. I don't know which task I should undertake. I don't have a sense of calling right now. My vocation doesn't seem apparent, but that does not make me a meaningless person. Because right in front of me, there's someone, there's something with whom or with which I can interact. I can honor that person or that situation, that place or that object, and I can give my love to it. Nothing can ever prevent me from giving my love to something or someone or someplace. Nothing can stop me from doing that." That is a choice. It's a behavior. It is an action. I can choose not to do it. But I can choose to do it, to give my self and my love in that way to bless and call forth the good in someone or something else. And when I choose to do it, it sets up a momentum. I choose to do it, and I choose to do it again, and after a while, it doesn't matter whether there is a call or not. I'm creating my own calling, moment by moment.

Well, our world is rich in callings and in summonings. John once said, "I don't like to prophesy because it focuses your attention in a specific direction, on a specific event. Then, because you are looking in that direction, you will miss what happens in the other directions. I'd much rather you pay attention to the moment and that you be poised and alert 360 degrees, in all directions. Things are happening all around you, all the time that are shaping your future. You can participate in them, but only if you are aware of them."

The same thing can be said about the call. Calls are all around us. We are never bereft of calls. But sometimes we just have to be poised and alert and aware in all directions to listen and to perceive them. We have to recognize that some calls come as whispers, some calls come in very ordinary ways. If we want to hear the big call, we cannot ignore the little ones. After all, the call that comes with a little "c" may be every bit as important, and may in fact be the foundation that allows us to receive the call with a capital "C."

About The Author

David Spangler lives in the Northwest, is married and has four children. Since 1965, he has worked clairvoyantly and intuitively with a group of non-physical beings from the inner worlds of spirit. They identified themselves as being part of an inner school whose purpose was to explore and develop a spiritual teaching around the process of incarnation. This teaching is intended to empower incarnate persons living in the physical world—individuals such as you and me—to lead lives of greater blessing and capacity and to be sources of blessing and service for the world as a whole. From 1970-1973, David was a co-director of the Findhorn Foundation Community in Northern Scotland. In 1974 he co-founded the Lorian Association, a non-profit spiritual educational organization, and continues to work with it today.

About The Publisher

Lorian Press is a private, for profit business which publishes works approved by the Lorian Association. Current titles can be found on the Lorian website www.lorian.org.

The Lorian Association is a not-for-profit educational organization. Its work is to help people bring the joy, healing, and blessing of their personal spirituality into their everyday lives. This spirituality unfolds out of their unique lives and relationships to Spirit, by whatever name or in whatever form that Spirit is recognized.

For more information, go to www.lorian.org.

CPSIA information can be obtained
at www.ICGtesting.com
Printed in the USA
FSOW01n0133211015
12391FS